Small Words

SHEARSMAN

95 & 96

SUMMER 2013

EDITED BY
TONY FRAZER

Shearsman magazine is published in the United Kingdom by
Shearsman Books Ltd
50 Westons Hill Drive, Emersons Green, BRISTOL BS16 7DF

Registered office: 30-31 St James Place, Mangotsfield, Bristol BS16 9JB
(this address not for correspondence)

www. shearsman.com

ISBN 978-1-84861-286-0
ISSN 0260-8049

Subscriptions and single copies

Current subscriptions—covering two double-issues, each around 108 pages, cost
£14 in the UK, £17 for the rest of Europe (including the Republic of Ireland), and
£19 for the rest of the world. Longer subscriptions may be had for a pro-rata higher
payment, which insulates purchasers from further price-rises during the
term of the subscription. North American customers will find that buying single
copies from online retailers in the USA will be cheaper than subscribing. £19
equates to about $30 at the time we went to press. The reason for this is that
overseas postage rates in the UK have risen significantly in the past 12 months.

Back issues from nº 63 onwards (uniform with this issue)—cost £8.50/$13.50
through retail outlets. Single copies can be ordered for £8.50, post-free, direct from
the press, through the Shearsman online store, or from bookstores in the UK and
the USA. Earlier issues, from 1 to 62, may be had for £3 each, direct from the press,
where they are still available, but contact us for prices for a full, or partial, run.

Submissions

Shearsman operates a submissions-window system, whereby submissions are only
accepted during the months of March and September, when selections are
made for the October and April issues, respectively. Submissions may be sent
by mail or email, but email attachments—other than PDFs—are not accepted.
We aim to respond within 2–3 months of the window's closure.

The next issue will be guest-edited by Kelvin Corcoran.

CONTENTS

Letters on Cézanne

Rilke said when he went to the Salon d'Automne
with Mathilde Vollmoeller to see the Cézannes
or perhaps it was Mathilde who said it and Rilke
wrote about it in one of those letters to his wife,
letters describing days of rain and going every day
to see the Cézannes, that the colour of his paintings,
each colour knowing every other colour in a
perpetual dialogue and exchange, that the colours
blended in the air around them, mixed into a neutral
grey, an atmosphere of equipose, almost velvet like—
the black and white only defining the limits of his
wide-open palette. It should be the same with us:
the Yes balancing out the No, Joy calming Despair
without cancellation: a day of sun and a day of rain.

The Theory of Touch

One theory was that the sense of handling—each apple
cupped in his palm and every colour weighed
so it became the thing itself—the tabletop, the pear—
one theory was that this caressing light across a wall,
this reaching out to feel each surface, sprung from phobia:
at school a boy had pushed him down the stairs
so even as an old man his son would have to say
'You'll forgive me father if I take your arm.'

Even in his final year when Émile Bernard reached to help him
on uneven ground, Cézanne cried out and shook him off.
I'm sated with touch. Last night I touched your face,
your arms, your chest as if touching would prove
some use against the the coming loss; as if I'd keep you
like he kept those—how many?—apples on a box.

4

Thought Path

I made a round of stones,
uneven stones,
    so I could walk

    the needles in a circling
path of thought.
    Pine trees, rough as broken

    masonry, leant up
among the shadows.
    I was like someone who goes

    into a shop, lifts down a vase
or a statuette of Pan,
    then puts it back. I said out loud,

    'Pine cones'—I bent my neck
to look: pine logs waiting
    for winter fires, holly oaks

    and rock roses with all their
petals gone. A bird
    seemed to shake a rattle

    for me to keep in step, while
another sang the same
    upward-sliding note. I was just

    about to stop when a voice
(not my voice in my throat)
    said softly *please ... please ...*

The Squirrel Sutra

Walking to the water trough
I stopped to see a squirrel stop,
a red squirrel drinking at the tap.

Hearing me it climbed the first
thin branches of a pine, then looked
to see if I was any kind of threat.

And as I stood a blackcap settled
on a branch, then hummingbird-like
seemed to stop midair while

the Yellow King with his horde
of hungry ghosts, the White King
surrounded by clelestial musicians,

the Red King with his entourage
of kumbhandas and fever spirits,
and the Green King took their stand.

Tamar Yoseloff

Wing Mirror

The ravine is a tangle of thorns, hubcaps, all the jagged edges of the night; kids scare each other shitless, drink and fuck until the blue light ghosts the trees. The ravine is a scar, a wound that opens wide, close to the burial sites of Escorts laced with rust; wing mirrors, eyes that never shut. Secrets stuck in the mud rise to the surface in rain: the fire extinguished, the party finished. Time to leave.

The ravine is a scar, a wound, a jagged secret. Kids party, drink fire, fuck in the mud; rust like shit sticks to the surface of hubcaps. Ghosts escort them to the edge of the burial site, mirror the night: blue light extinguished in rain. They rise on tangled wings laced with thorns, their eyes are shut. The ravine is open wide, never scared. The trees close their leaves.

The ravine is shit, a fucking thorn in the eye. Kids wing it, tangled up and blue. They drink until their secrets are buried, score surface wounds on hubcaps, scare the ghosts wide from the trees. They fire open night, the party never shuts. In the rain and mud they lace their scars with rust. They rise and leave before their time is finished. Extinguished. The mirror's jagged edge sticks them in its sights. The ravine closes the light.

The ravine is edged with a light surface of rain. Mirrors rust; the fire extinguished like a ghost. Shitty site to be buried: stuck in the drink, in the mud, like a hubcap. Don't tangle with the night; time is a party that finishes in a ravine; out of the blue your escort's fucked off, and you're a thorn in a wing. Don't be scared, kids. Never rise to the secret that shuts the eyes. Wounds close, but they leave scars.

Gatekeeper

I am your port of entry, the point of no return,
you yield to my kludgy touch,
the Magic Fingers you can't switch off. I am a screen

for your sins, discreet, like a Venetian blind you shut
to kill the light. I am night,
starless, sharp with little cries; you navigate through touch.

I am the Goddess Kali of a thousand fingers,
I'll stroke, stroke until a scream
rises from your gut, the beast unfurled, a masterpiece

of hurt. I am your Painted Lady, your Queen of Spain,
a wing in the rake of thorns;
I cling to you like grave clothes, the suit you'll never shake.

I am the circus freak, the double act of one. Gone
through a gash, flash in the pan;
it doesn't last, the searing lash of pain, slash of skin,

peek-a-boo of blood. I'm in the driver's seat, the scent
of burning flesh, gasoline
quivering my nostrils; I'm full-throttle towards the wall.

I am the swallow in your throat, hollow in your heart,
deep rut of the furrowed field.
I slay without a sound, here inside my velvet box.

The Glass Enigma

This window, icy to the finger, clear
almost as non-existence, has allowed
the sun or stars through since before the Black
Death struck. Each pane's now slightly thicker at
the base thinning towards the top for glass
is not a solid nor a liquid yet
keeps qualities of both to fox us with
translucent mystery. Quick centuries
permitting moonshine and excluding hail
saw tiny bubbles rise the fraction of
an inch while gravity contrived to drag
impurities with hardly any weight
down just as slowly, as remorselessly.
Captives who happened to have diamonds
about their person scratched surnames or poems
in spidery letters sometimes signing off
with a crude coat-of-arms catching white light
to prove identities post mortem (theirs)
and challenge time though less successfully.

Scattershot

for Lynn

1.

Now there now here
ripping through leaves
to whine off from
the lead shoulders
of naiads stuck
round a fountain

No ricochet
whenever puffs
of pinkish dust
leave dark thumbprints
pinged at random
on four brick walls

All that in some
other garden
alien to these
hushed paths where crude
target practice
is unheard of

2.

Bullets unformed
from fire and iron
occur and aim
in legend lost
conjecture late
dreams or elsewhere

Manned when by whom
in wonder meant
to graze their prey
and disappear
once motives aren't
learnt till later

Passing from air
through air to air
with an effect
of colder light-
ning striking here
now there then where

The Monkey-Rope

We know Dante put his friends
in hell. It's easy, and probably right
from the balcony, floating over
the permanently unhorsed, a seeing
eye in the night of others. At first
hand, though, we feel ourselves: a bee sense
of what's been tried on the training ground,
raising you above, well, personal misery;
it comes to us already ground and
chipped and powdered and mixed and sliced,
but between the whale and the ship
there's an end that's ours, and while
on the shore of exceeding caution someone
plays the galleried scourge of vantage, living
but dust-capped even at the best of times
he only flounders in another kind of belly,
sponsored perhaps, as the labour
continues in-between. This isn't boxing
where raw talent can get a result,
but looking at you across the focus of
the camera sat ostentatiously
crow-like over the steel palings
of that white building for our own
protection—that scarf is nice on you,
I feel the faintest almost of your touch,
and you're all I can really love. And though
the best way to make a small fortune
is to start with a large one, through tocsins
the helmet lamps lighting the streets
after the wild work of the *barricas* show again
an anatomy for heavy lifting, suffering
but tenacious, constituting, rising
like living bread.

22 Minutes Ago Near Acton

Reports in the reporting season, the warm
averages of observer status, your
publisher's war crimes. What's searchable
is already there: William of Moerbeke
translating Aristotle de verbo in verbo,
a silence on what eludes, pleasure filed
by the ought of seeing with other, tagged
afterthoughts. Outside they sang 'O take me
to Michael's Rock, then,' begging to be clad
in an atmosphere of sanctuary,
but in the italicized dream of this language
sponsored by your little electronic soul
no amount of elegy will restore the shade
where your furniture was. We have seen
the word gadget become obsolete. Is
a career in love-making the only reply
to the false maps of feedback?
Should I compromise on quality?
The brain lock trumps vagabondage,
which from these clerestories sounds
like a daring manner of conference table.
There was virtually nothing to identify
the aircraft. Click here to talk to a Mormon.

Sonnet

Rainbow missing on louring sky,
a seagull strolls through a big puddle
overlooking the cathedral because of you,
because of my hangover

Man vs nature, time vs space,
the New Critics loved figures of the Incarnation
(Birds go by like cars:
with my alcoholism and your good looks, etc.)

The itch of my mouth-side molars,
the giant cartoon ladybird in the waiting room
Angela Merkel thinks I'm at work

The last two speakers of Ayapaneco
refuse to talk to each other, lady, but
the passing stranger is often taken for a deity

GERALDINE CLARKSON

golden opportunity wet streets

give his side a golden opportunity to move
each passing minute seemingly misses one
—if you have
anaconda, or ball python, pine—

opportunity to read what everyone
open in the mouth and good
could see. For one year flowers shone
blooming in Sweden at the end of May.

Assigned to the city of Spokane,
we are over the charred or crumbling
rain-wet street. I stood at the War
(for seconds). Lilies sued for peace

each passing minute seemingly missing one
while lilac snow milled wisdom in city ruins.

A List Poem

i)
Archive, ballot, Blue book,
card file, census, checklist,
contents, diptych, index,
invoice, ledger, line-up,
listing, memo, menu,
outline, panel, program,
record, Red book, roll call,
roster, schedule, series,
table, tally, wish list

ii)
Almanac, army list, bulletin,
catalogue, cadaster, checker roll,
classify, chronicle, civil list,
clergy list, dictionary, Domesday book,
inventory, itemise, laundry list,
lexicon, muster roll, manifest,
numerate, register, rolodex,
service list, shopping list, specialise,
specify, syllabus, tabulate

iii)
Arrangement, directory, prospectus,
statistics, synopsis, thesaurus…

JOHN LATTA

Outlandishness and Euphemism

Against empire's vain memorial to its own human loss, scrupulous in its incommensurability: scrappy outlandishness, horse-nonsense, and bunk. Braying factotum, wiener pierced by a stick. Vanity of the base human commitment to a thuggery of 'us.' Baton twirling girls high-kneeing it down Main. Fatty the pursed embouchures of the shrewd liars, the Aeolus-flatterers harping for corporate gain. A sentimental gin-sop lapses gamely into prayer. A 'common' soldier with blood-colored epaulettes rehearses a story made retail-ready by euphemism. Pure blood-urge of manufactured urgency. Prodding the vulgar to accept some particular of *a priori* 'evil,' some make-ready of the final real 'impossible either to correct or analyze.' Up in the aerial vault the chimney swifts teeter and sail, teeter and sail and thieve. On the dying green lawn, two rabbits, dog-spooked, freeze.

Essays and Nettles

Some mock essays to do and the tender green nettles (lopped off with a Bowie knife in a prickly fit of florilegium'd ascertainment and culling) to parboil and a murderous sigh of prank dejectedness to interpose between summary and end: isn't that enough? Enough of too corpulent trots and jag-engineered reminiscences, enough of 'beyond the ken of the local' *sub rosa* hoots? Stumped by a word, I like to mouth it out *pianissimo*, or grind it down into use 'with inexorable jaw.' Against cloying invect and the perniciousness of Cape Mootch (a vodka): 'sing high and aloofe.' Against putrescent kissinesses and the *lie doggo* vernaculars of Regents Park (a park): 'pour the sacred boonion.' Some not-so-pricey comeuppance is in the works, some 'economy of meaning' that'll burst *all* drawers. Drawers: 'apparently a term of low origin, usually restricted to underclothing worn next the skin.' Drawers made up of 'stuffe of mockadoo.'

Lash and Foment

To mosey down along a various stretch of river unequalled, freighting up a satchel with the debris it hauls along in its opaque and shiny and moveable girth, or the indigestible toss it discharges in eddies. Like a snake or a sentence or a briefing. To mimeo 'off' a small batch of collateral works in mulberry-colored inks with the nostril-scouring odor of some frankly carcinogenic ketone. *Melius nesciendo scitur* means 'he is better known by not being known.' Thus there is no brutish ontological need for any *particular* trajectory to ensue, nor for anyone's discourse to declare itself part of the lash and foment of sheer reason. Indefatigable reason, like Bakelite or Formica. Each telling of this henceforth is irremediably likened to mine, as if I were a thing sculpted out of Plasticine, a modeling clay invented by William Harbutt in Bath in 1897, Play-Doh's rump precursor. Down where the dam assuages the river's outpour by means of a temporary impediment, allowing it pause to muster a fit next denied, I stand ankle-deep in this irreproachable urgency like a knot, or a code. The river washes the putty-colored rocks, and the putty-colored chubs.

Valence and Register

What if the sentient outpouring itself becomes an anesthetic, a *cauchemar* of rectitude in lieu of the bare-shouldered moll with a blade, or the derringer in a debutante's hand? The pliable *I* with its artifice of sincerity, the lascivious *Q* with its tongue hanging out like a tease. I overdo each thing with a mannerist's clatter, novel-prepping for no reason. There's little enough to go on here, or to go on *about*. I finished up planning for my end at the Zenith Days sponsored by Acme. Here on out it's going to be all earth's own 'reechy kisses' in the summer downpours, and Craven A's in a box, nutty and sweet. A cardinal barks out its radical valence of 'Cheer cheer, what cheer?' off the rooftop's spindly antenna, a wren pours its soda'd song into the nostril-pinching and sour whiskey'd air. Repeating the old penumbral maneuvers *ad infinitum*, each in a different register. That moll's got a run.

Distaff and Forklift

Nothing like lyrical pomp to undo a storyteller's zone, its wholly general ratifying clench. Like a distaff with 'a bit of slub depending.' *Ryder.* Meaning a yarn poorly spun, one with bumps and irregularities at intervals. The day refusing to compose itself, noticeably entrenched under an onslaught of lousy weather. The sere thunderclaps of my spent youth: like a skid's worth of boards splaying down off a forklift. A tall grass crayfish hole the size of a man's boot back by the artesian well, its constant watery rope lank and stuttery. Cold-numbed fingers pinched number. Memory's form is like what Picasso called Cubism's: a 'sum of destructions.' My numbered days: a vireo in the sun-slathered reaches of oak saying *'finish up, finish up.'*

éire

é
éir
éireé
éireéir
éireééire
éireéir
ireéi
reé
e

abcTdef
kjAiAhg
lRmTnRo
ArAqRpA
sRtAuRv
zAyAxw
zyxTwvu
pqArAst
oRnTmRl
ghAiAjk
fedTcba

Fields of Blue and White

1.

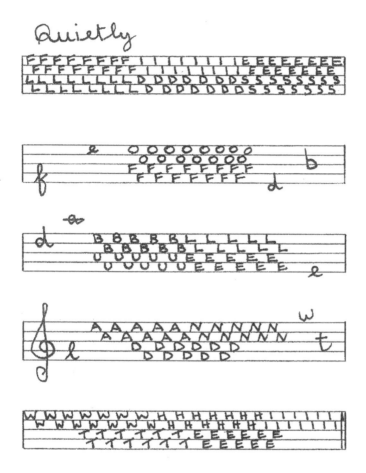

Fields of Blue and White

2.

FFFFFFIIIIIIEEEEEELLLLLLDDDDDDSSSSSS
FFFFFFIIIIIIEEEEEELLLLLLDDDDDDSSSSSS
FFFFFFIIIIIIEEEEEELLLLLLDDDDDDSSSSSS
FFFFFFIIIIIIEEEEEELLLLLLDDDDDDSSSSSS
OOOOOOFFFFFFBBBBBBLLLLLLUUUUUUEEEEEE
OOOOOOFFFFFFBBBBBBLLLLLLUUUUUUEEEEEE
OOOOOOFFFFFFBBBBBBLLLLLLUUUUUUEEEEEE
OOOOOOFFFFFFBBBBBBLLLLLLUUUUUUEEEEEE
AAAAAAAAAAAANNNNNNNNNNNNDDDDDDDDDDDD
AAAAAAAAAAAANNNNNNNNNNNNDDDDDDDDDDDD
AAAAAAAAAAAANNNNNNNNNNNNDDDDDDDDDDDD
AAAAAAAAAAAANNNNNNNNNNNNDDDDDDDDDDDD
WWWWWWWWHHHHHHHHIIIIIIIIITTTTTTTEEEEEE
WWWWWWWWHHHHHHHHIIIIIIIIITTTTTTTEEEEEE
WWWWWWWWHHHHHHHHIIIIIIIIITTTTTTTEEEEEE
WWWWWWWWHHHHHHHHIIIIIIIIITTTTTTTEEEEEE

Towards the Light

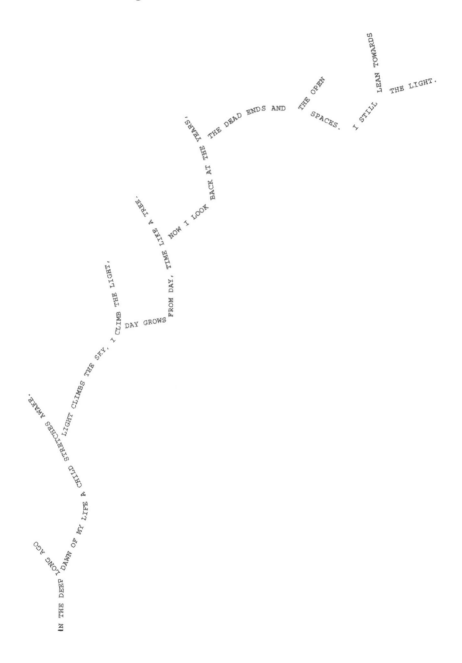

IN THE DEEP DAWN OF MY LIFE A CHILD STRETCHES AWAKE. LIGHT CLIMBS THE SKY, I CLIMB THE LIGHT, DAY GROWS FROM DAY, TIME LIKE A TREE. NOW I LOOK BACK AT THE YEARS, THE DEAD ENDS AND THE OPEN SPACES. I STILL LEAN TOWARDS THE LIGHT.

Tom Bamford

next time
wear the skin of the six-eyed bird

you during this not
die but feel a lukewarm breath still
bed and the
dawn shard
remember. how glad your friends do not go
before you how
away your friends are
not on your side and
where the disorganisation is from
a book to be
fresh after all is
        peace without conscious
ness the bles
sing of hunger
        the bright space left
still
        the song and police erase the streets leaving payment re
lieved by a nest of starlings/
in mind's hungry amber
light walk peeping in
bushes where they
have gone but
is regardless and in her eternity/

ketamine earth

this no time for but inconveniently the
epic heart not with barricades must
beat in leaves to
pulse dirt cons
tellations to
soak mixed earth and sky in self reliance to
walk past where signs are
exchanging tendrils making
acceptable where the hearth's
crystals link our brains / trees / phones in
making open the decay of

in the moss the wall's lines
deregulating the sky with colour
coded LUXURY a
young video paint bleed between people and objects the
regret in his voice like a jewel case at the ease of it
all going
in diamond lines hang dewy in
the lush corridor and trampling the wet
profile walking
past good double glazing / mould
in white plastic / blue fur / battery mould and chlorine /
i hate this:

thank god for dead volcanoes that they shower us in concerts as we
bask in their reticence to harm us; thank the gods that have turned
themselves into buried screens blessing with their electric blood /
empty airports / empty forests / korgs
buried in snow / helicopters overhead /

JEN CRAWFORD

from Soft Shroud

smashed scattering   bulwarks

                            blond splinters whirl

'someone's coming out for our furniture   unhinged gate & circle
drive bursting

feet swollen seats   face-up imploring
  'sky   sky   honey the roof's gone   honey the walls oh soak
                                        your ankles
                   look out   perimetres
fully ponding
                                     look

nestmate recognition

curled   thorax

                                              hovers over smashed

   lip s   combed cliff   we were hiding and the sun

honey sliding   over the cell   to

                                   hive

under the surface is warm

                enteric brain, cat-minded body brain soft is
                    several inches of warm   under the
    surface   a bubble
silver egg with a wet chin

                        thigh remembers ending down
         in chilly weed

in chilly dark   above is a mirror ball brain   turning
silver in the

warmth where the sun light can
              between the stump both giving and
      receiving

        fish-minded thigh-brain turn   a ganglion can

SAM SAMPSON

Doubled Lexicon

for Gustaf Sobin

the horizon

     O

pens

the circle

     Sobin

circles the expanse   expands dirt

          distributes

     the liquescent

ellipse   :

          the glittering......... geometric design

of the glass headed light

---

     two in-

complete oblong drops

     the pond of the Olive Tree

          O

     pens

the mirror

shadows swing the windrow

:

   ground

      rocky outcrops: composed of chalk and green sand
                     composed of shelly sandstone cliffs

     layers, over-
laying clays, marly macigno
                        the lignite field

---

     erasure links the sentence

sentences the

pause

      recesses the sun

   O

       pens

the corridor

  (structure up-
     dates   a staircase disappears...

            ceramic wind chimes
charred grape seeds
         Ionian soft paste
   pinkish circular bands)

       registers
as rectangular frames
       the utterance

awkward   doubled lexicon
  two diagonal lines

          at right angles
    the child centre   it-

  self   dead-centre

     O

---

pens

the footnote

        calibrates...
    passage

caresses   the eye-

lid-en————————————
   closed circumference   deeply etched

      ligated   to the (be-
clouded)   presence of identical blocks
   printed in raw clay.

Erasure

for Don Binney, artist, conservationist

history in a nearby tree
isolated sightings ~~(aligned by absence):~~ ———— ~~huia extinct~~ ————

Féileacán *

Attach all meaning to fire

years of blown off candles
years of burning in with no instruction out

old records that don't function new
inside an iconic city with no reflection above

a Prometheus with no place to place a plague

The ongoing tempest
the outgoing oracle
the splashing oar

the edge of biologic implants.

Butterfly [Irish]

Dílleachtlann *

a ponytail picks up shells
weighs them in one hand
to estimate value

Inside the sea aspens of bizarre fish
roll around their spin to entangle you

I lay down towel
let the waves battle in
things that lived inside my two grandmothers
like stones collected meticulously
might appear again in unsuspected pressures

I have to art-create the creation
with possession of increments
measuring inside chemistry tubes
passway letters in different shapes
dilettante acts

I'm my own fish
a human foreground.

Orphanage [Irish]

Cláirseach *

for Guisy

Unhung the small masks
your eyes are hidden in carbon

you are hiding something from

>   Dress in a deity's flops?
>   Hungry the unfed?
>   Noise as a flute?
>   Unravel?

She looks at

beside the river bank
the unbroken
seducing
brutal

She stands wearing a

She descends into the middle of the river
She's bathing, the water is
Her hair floats

>   hear the tambourine?
>   lower spine drains
>   clarinet drowns
>   blue emerald
click-clock
you are hiding something from

the hidden gets lost
and the lost gets gotten.

* *Harp* [Irish]

35

μπαγιάτικos

this is it   the path that leads to the source of the river
is there a technical name for that?   you see it i think
not quite as you imagined it   glass conch mineral gem
      with mud and memory mint

we've been walking a lifetime   me with the map you folded
into a rocket   the cities you blasted out of your window
the window you climbed from come nightfall   before jumping
      through all the hoops

did you look?   vaya si te ha costado   your heart in shreds
your voice fleeing disorientated up cliffs and under bridges
scaling madness but who says there's no kindness left
      in the seventh circle of hell?

the breeze is playing tricks this afternoon   oxygen to please
the pain   and this path that takes the wolverine
out of every false start   it's making me hungry now   see?
for the berries crushed under your feet

επεξεργάζομαι

she opens her mouth and excerpts from the black box
drift out   lipstick beside months under the sea

unlike in dreams it's hard to tell faces from sounds
posture is an invisible clue   instead a barrage of metal speak

that's what the experts are there for   to glue the syntax
of cracks   pronounce a fuselage   gas or mechanical

fault   imagine pilots not knowing dexterous from sinister
up from doom   ?   they gauze her last words

among the sadness of the sea bed   she thinks of the doors
she left unlocked back home   (this comes through)

unhurried about what burglars might take   there's nothing
to take   it's more what they might put into the house

Isobel Armstrong

Glass Symphony: Kristallnacht

FIRST MOVEMENT

long-stemmed green wine glasses
fine-cut little glasses for port
filigreed champagne glasses

my symphony and song
      crystal symphony
      crystal song
           cry
the sounds of transparency
as hollow glasses sing   in air
raisedringing against each other
delight ringsinging
hollowing out sound
      crystal cry
breaking forever in waves
that soon will be
millions of miles old
the shape of transparency   breaking
there is no outside to sound
no other side   no beyond
ringsinging in

sensuous riddles of glass

hard but
     translucency is its shape   clear and shining
outlines made solid all out of light
and emptiness

silent harmonics of light
play inside and outside transparency
light breaks   and reverberates

38

through quiet   intransigent   limpid sides
sound one   single   exact note
a glass will fall to pieces

and what if
someone inverted the flask
and is pouring out all the light
and emptiness?

...pulling a handle which opened up the dining room table,
revealing underneath a leaf which, when put in place, served to
bridge the distance between the two halves of the table, so that
all the guests could be accommodated. Then I had been given
permission to help set the table. In doing so, not only was I
honoured by having utensils like lobster forks and oyster knives
pass through my hands; but even the familiar everyday utensils
called into service—the long-stemmed green wine glasses, the
fine-cut little glasses for port, the filigreed champagne glasses,
the silver saltcellars shaped like little tubs, the heavy metal carafe-
stoppers in the form of gnomes or animals—all had a festive air
about them. Finally, I was allowed to position, on one of the many
glasses at each place-setting, the card which announced where
that particular guest was to sit.[1]

his Berlin childhood when his father's white shirt gleamed like a
mirror welcoming guests
long-stemmed green wine glasses
fine-cut little glasses for port
filigreed champagne glasses
carafe stoppers

each guest's card   by the many glasses at each place setting
who sat at table but so crowded there was no room for death

---

[1] From Walter Benjamin's *Berlin Childhood*. Walter Benjamin began to revise his
Berlin Childhood in 1938, the year of Kristallnacht, the night of broken glass

*Here reigned a type of furniture that, having capriciously
incorporated styles of ornament from different centuries, was
thoroughly imbued with itself and its own duration. Poverty could
have no place in these rooms, where death itself had none. There was
no place in them to die; and so their occupants died in sanatoriums,
while the furniture went directly to a dealer as soon as the estate was
settled. In these rooms death was not provided for. That is why they
appeared so cosy by day and became the scene of bad dreams by night.*

bad dreams by night

someone filled the carafe up with light
and stoppered it up
and now the light has congealed in it

impenetrable   a still clear lump in the sun
dust lies on the outside

death was not provided for

**after the wedding was over
we danced at the best hotel
the windows misted over
as we danced so it chanced
to palm court musicians and canapés
while portly lugubrious   and slow
our mother was waltzed in the style of an earlier phase
from three decades ago
backs arched in manoeuvres once made to amaze
and our children played by the orchestra   we talked   and it all
          went well
the bride and the groom were so happy and...**

*breathe on a window pane
a sigh made visible
haze on a chill surface is
the history of breath*

time precipitate
          in vapour
                    for a moment
                              only seen by
dimming the glass and the eye

vapour clears resolved
momentarily to tears   or
brushed by an impatient hand
blurs to a watery residue   so
the eye sees through
a mark that its own body's made

warm breath and cold converge
a living mist forms
where a glass-blower's exhalation
hardened into transparency
he left his mark
informing blankness
with an invisible history
lived by emptying out his lungs

one breath seen through another
matching air with air
now the gazer's solitude is over
the past's cold breath repairs   except
for the window pane's syllogism
that declares
there is still more to utter
what these words make visible and suppress
the unsaid words for die and death

'Mazel Tov!'
under the canopy
after the ceremony
the Rabbi's reading
a fragile glass
wrapped in an impeccable napkin

was crushed by an impeccable leather shoe
we peered at the sharply creased trousers
the groom's solemn face
how could they decide the groom and his bride
what this fracture was for?
we were crying though as we cried 'Mazel Tov'

did they once dash the glass to the ground   both of them perhaps

sliversplintered
silvershattered
light glints
on shards
irremediably
splitsplintered   forced
into the flesh

is that it   love's forever piercing
or

fractured light and glass
together
broken to infinity
strange bond from breaking
the split that multiplies
love's everlasting
fracturing matter and light
forever
or

nothing can be sole or whole
that has not been rent   well ... there's that too
or

the always exodus
the arch of Titus
reared to assert the razing
of Jerusalem's Second Temple

crushed under foot
Hadrian finished it off
Sliversplintered
shards

or

and all those wedding guests   in
half a glass of wine   reflecting
inverted people walking about
in golden fluid
half way up a goblet
crowding a liquid nether world
flushed blue and red
to ceiling lights beneath them

quieter upper space
of empty glass
films
refractions   vaguer lights   apart
cut off by golden liquid

from smokers drinkers   talkers
eaters of canapés
suspended from a liquid surface
severing upper and nether space

hard to see the logic of
blurred images
crossed and recrossed by themselves

easy to see all these people
sitting upside down   drinking   eating
latkes
lox
gefilte
knish
condensed alive here…

must connect somehow   but
what are you staring for
the children ask
what are you doing peering
so hard at your glass
mad Mum
this is only wine I say
think of a beer glass
all those facets
compounding prismatic fragments
bits and pieces
of so many worlds
mad Mum

Crack
I found an elegant line one day
terminating in imperceptible transparency
it was two lines or four
edges cut in the clarity
accurate matching severance
held apart in the tense glass   and two
internal planes facing across a fissure of air
reciprocal landscapes   ruin of such precision
each glacial hollow fits
what it was hollowed from
multiple splinterage
corresponds with translucent scree

a gash in the skin   eager membrane
thread and filament will bodge
up the tissue somehow and stop
the scarlet drops
but this is a clean cut, an integral fault
crack

*Shadow*Shadow
a drained glass
has shed its slanting copy

away on to the table
where things are made their double

tenebrae for a form
displaced into a shadow

concentric gleams of luster show
in sediments of light
things that are not there
or which cannot appear
until secreted layers of radiance
show   *in the flux of a shadow*
residues hardened long ago

it does not match but it is warm
holding things impossible to see
except by seeing double

except in an ellipse of shade
contours made of light
spilled on to a table

tenebrae

filigree champagne glasses
green long stemmed wine glasses
little glasses for port fine cut

bad dreams *death not provided for*   *tenebrae*

echo o o o   singingin ….insinging ….in
millions of miles old

black adagio

grinding lenses and working
on hate's logic
bending light

physics of adiaphane
making translucency visible
no nerves in glass
refracting love and hate through one another
hater and lover
grinding the dry lexicon
for hate's black voracious libido
dark images of a dark adagio
to hate
you have to create
dioptric images bent by light

Spinoza Lexicon 1[2]

Each thing ... strives to persevere in its being.
Striving ... *essence of the thing.*

he saw the 'I' in desire

Envy is hatred itself.

Men are by nature envious ... men are naturally inclined to hate
and envy.

every kind of sadness, and especially what frustrates longing.

we call it good because we desire it.

---

[2] Baruch Spinoza, *Ethics*, adapted from the translation by Edwin Curley.

this joy and sadness are species of love and hate.

Every kind of sadness

Each thing ... strives to persevere in its being.

Spinoza Lexicon 2

hatred itself.

naturally inclined to hate and envy.
Every kind of sadness
            envy   sadness

joy and sadness   species of love and hate
        sadness   hate
When the mind imagines its own lack of power it is saddened by it ...
                                  saddened by

Spinoza Refractions

1
He who imagines what he hates to be affected with sadness with sadness
will rejoice; if, on the other hand, he should imagine it to be affected
with joy, he will be saddened ... be saddened saddened
the image in the lover of the loved thing's joy the loved thing's
joy the loved thing's joy aids his mind's striving, that is ... affects
the lover with joy lover with joy ... except the being whom he
imagines the thing he loves to love ... Because he imagines that
what he loves affects with joy what he hates, and also because he
is forced to join the image of the thing he loves the image of the
thing he loves the image of the thing he loves to the image of the
thing he hates.

2

*If someone begins to hate the thing he loved ... begins to hate the thing
he loved ... begins to hate ... this hate this hate will be the greater
greater as the love before was greater ... as the love before was greater
... was greater*
 apart from the sadness which was the cause of the hate, another
arises from the fact that he loved the thing ... sadness   from the
fact that he loved the thing he loved the thing he loved.

3

*The joy which arises from our imagining that a thing we hate is
destroyed a thing we hate is destroyed is destroyed, or affected with some
other evil, does not occur without some sadness of mind sadness of mind
sadness...*
the more so, the more so the greater this affect was in the thing
loved the thing loved ... insofar as a thing is affected with sadness
sadness, it is destroyed destroyed, and the more so the more so the
greater the sadness sadness sadness with which it is affected ... he
who imagines what he loves to be affected with sadness, will also
be affected with sadness with sadness with sadness, and the more
so, the greater this affect was in the thing loved the thing loved the
thing loved.

4

*If we imagine someone to affect with joy a thing we hate a thing we
hate a thing we hate, we shall be affected with hate hate hate toward
him also...*
If we imagine someone to affect with joy a thing we love a thing
we love a thing we love, we shall be affected with love with love
with love towards him. If, on the other hand, we imagine him to
affect the same thing with sadness sadness sadness...

5

*We strive to affirm, concerning what we hate what we hate what we
hate, whatever we imagine to affect it with sadness sadness sadness,
and on the other hand, to deny to deny to deny whatever we imagine to
affect it with joy...*
We strive to affirm, concerning ourselves and what we love what
we love, whatever we imagine to affect with joy to affect with joy

joy joy ourselves and what we love love. On the other hand, we strive to deny whatever we imagine affects with sadness ourselves or what we love with sadness ourselves or what we love what we love.

6

If we imagine that someone enjoys something that only one can possess, we shall strive to bring it about that he does not possess it not possess it not possess it not possess ... Joy posits the existence of the joyous thing, ... and the more so, the greater the joy is conceived to be ... Joy posits the existence of the joyous thing, ... and the more so the more so, the greater the greater the joy is conceived to be. Joy posits the existence of the joyous thing. Joy joy joy.

7

He who hates someone who hates someone will strive strive strive to do evil do evil to him ... As far as we can, we strive to imagine, above all others, the thing we love above all others the thing we love the thing we love. We strive to make the thing we love affected with joy for us ... affected with joy with joy affected.

8

He who imagines he is hated by someone, and believes he has given the other no cause for hate no cause for hate, will hate hate hate the other in return. ... When we love we love a thing like ourselves, we strive, as far as we can, to bring it about that it loves us in return loves us in return loves us.

9

If someone has been affected with joy or sadness by someone of a class, or nation, different from his own, and this joy or sadness is accompanied by the idea of that person as its cause, under the universal name of the class or nation, he will love or hate, not only that person, but everyone of the same class or nation.

If someone has been affected with joy or sadness by someone of a class, or nation, different from his own, and this joy or sadness is accompanied

49

by the idea of that person as its cause, under the universal name of the
class or nation, he will love or hate, not only that person, but everyone of
the same class or nation.

10
Hate is increased by being returned, but can be destroyed by love.
Then it will prevail over it and efface the hate from his mind.

Coda
When the mind imagines He who imagines he should imagine from our
imagining If we imagine whatever we imagine whatever we imagine
If we imagine. If we imagine … strives striving we strive we shall
strive He will strive … to be affected to be affected or affected to

The being whom he imagines Because he imagines the image the
image to imagine If we imagine If, on the other hand we imagine
we imagine we imagine he who imagines if we imagine if we
imagine aids his mind's striving we strive we strive We strive we
strive to affirm we strive to deny affects the lover with joy affected
with joy to affect to affect with joy affects with sadness is affected
it is affected to be affected be affected this affect

Lens
no nerves in it
burning-glass
germinating light
a piece of glass   without a will
flames without volition
consumed a sunny hill
that's blackened still

casually seeded
a crystal pulse
throbs to the sun
shard shattered windscreen
bottle in a fight
is all that's needed
the flat and convex surface

it would take a man hours to grind
fragment that fills up unseen
slowly with solid light
until it is too late
and it will propagate

a silent and inconscious thing
intensifying light without desire

the screaming of small animals
landscape's nerve ends
conflagration and fury
              screaming
scars green life to black
gums and balms weep
out of flaring vegetation
air suddenly visible as trembling flux
where trees and grasses shudder
fire seizes the red wind
and there's a hillside razed

a blackened hill
a broken fragment
without desire
a broken hill

but hate? but hate? hate's libido?

THIRD MOVEMENT
– SCHERZO SONNETS – THE NIGHT OF BROKEN GLASS

'Many knights came from afar to try their luck, but it was in vain
they attempted to climb the glass mountain.' The Glass Mountain.
A Polish Fairy Tale. Andrew Lang, *The Yellow Fairy Book*.

how did they get up it?
slithering-smooth glistening sides

clutching crystal-gnarled roots
slippery-glittering down
down sliding down glassy wastes
in a deep crevasse to rot with other bodies
impaled on broken spikes

for a cold unreachable lady
and golden apples
on sharp peaks

cut off a lynx's claws
thrust its spikes into the shrieking surface   gauge
out crystal grit
graze the screeching sides
(no nerves in glass)

got there in the end
dragged by a captured eagle
up the last shining cliffs
he cut its talons off

the shrieking bird's blood
ran down crystal ravines
he reached the lady
the golden apples   on the precipices
and frigid wastes

trampling   heavy boots   the dreaded   knock on the door [3]
there was a   knock   on the door
dreaded   bang   on the door   we froze   when we heard   the
knock on   the door   heavy
army boots on   stairs   stopped
outside the   door
loud knocking
sounded   so terribly   loud   to   us

---

[3] Lines commencing with "trampling" and concluding with "to take her father away" (p.54) are phrases and sentences quoted sequentially from Gilbert Martin, *Kristallnacht: Prelude to Destruction*, Harper Perennial, 2007.

smash   ing furniture and mir   rors   ye   lling
mother's jewellery br   oke all the mi   r   rors
woken in the middle of the night burst into my room sc   reaming
sm   ashing the gla   ss on each picture
all the win   dows s   mashed
shat   tered gl   ass made it dangerous to
walk anywhere
awakened to the so   und of shatt   ering g   lass and loud shou   ts
rang the doorbells smas   hed the glas   s w   indows
b   roke in the soun   d of broke   n g   lass
win   d   ows were sm   ash   ed with rocks
gla   s   s front door was s   m   ash   ed b   ro   ke   n g   l   a   s   s
all over the floor corridor
I awoke from the sh   att   er   ing of gla   s   s

thrown   out of a window   and killed
not dare   to go near   a window
we women   watched   behind the curtains
wondering   how soon   they would   kill us
hid   in the   bathroom
under   the furniture

br   o   ke w   in   dows in nearly every Jewish shop
destroying wi   n   dows, goods
sm   a   shed sh   opwi   ndows
b   ro   ken g   l   ass wrecked goods all over the road

cra   sh   ing the shop win   d   ow of the bakery
s   m   ashing the wi   n   dows of jewellery shops
began to sm   as   h up the shops all around us
plate-gl   a   ss display wind   ow   s sh   at   tered
hurling stones through a shop win   do   w
throwing stones through the br   oke   n wind   o   w panes
the gla   s   s vitrine bevelled win   do   ws
plate glass wi   ndow   s lying in spl   in   ters
brok   e   n g   las   s everywhere
'why have they bro   ke   n that shop win   do   w?'

grand piano was hauled out on to the pavement
demolished with hatchets
                with hatchets
were beginning to move the piano scream
                        scream
an upright piano on to the balcony
smashing the balustrade
over the edge   nose-dived
a sickening crash
wooden casing broke away
a harp standing in the middle of the debris
                        middle of the debris
my mother's grand piano was in pieces
                was in pieces

Jewish
men away
Dachau arrested taken
away they never returned
arrested under armed guard to
day all Jewish men taken to

the Gestapo to take her father away

by the glass mountain
birds   flying easy through the uncoloured air   flying
easy through the limpid wind
will hurl into that   lucid obstruction   and
there's crashed feathers   bleeding   a muddle of death
bleeding   the indefatigable ones though
to force that shell of unseen hardness
knock with their tough yellow beaks   sagged skin
all stretched out   concentrating   tap
tap   tap   tap   Tap

FOURTH MOVEMENT
ANDANTE ELEGY

1 BROKEN GLASS

'I must turn this straw into gold if I wish to live' —Rumpelstiltskin

I must turn this glass to   put them together   this bright
        translucid debris
piecing edge to piercing edge
splinter by shard by sliver
sliver by splinter by shard   by sliver
by shard by fragment by flake by segment   by splinter
irrational splinter-shatter strata
scored with invisible striae sever
shard-splinter-sliver   fracture
sliver-splinter

always the caesura
where interstices of crack and fracture
start and shatter
edge from edge
translucid   bloody
where fingers run with blood

 there must be some logic to the breaking of glass
a science of shock and shattering
as there are monstrous rules
for maelstrom and moraine
the exact blow   the law of ruin
dictates a precise conchoidal fracture
patterns unbearable stress   sudden splitting   where
the golden bowl lies in pieces
integers of violence   where
the golden bowl lies in pieces

slash the moon's face
hatred surges beyond

sciences of shock and fracture
beyond   beyond
any ratio to depict hate's thrill, hate's ecstasy, hate's rapture
jouissance of the victim's fear   slash
the moon's face   slash
reflecting your own light
running with blood

come away
not here   not here
give over   trying to
redeem the piercing splinter in the heart
release translucency from pulverized matter
free invisible transparency buried in the primal sand and quartz
invert the science of shock and fracture
free
adiaphane   hyaline   and the sound of wings
from the night of the broken windows
come away

start over
where Los and his descendants laboured at the furnace
where a vitreus flux lethal-soft scarlet-viscous
lies ready   alive
for the makers
molten in the crucible
to be drawn to filaments
to be fused with the motion of light
to be rendered hollow by the pressure of breath
forming a contour from the ductile air
sigh-shaped
where
soft red heat disappears into glass
scarlet heat fades into transparency   and
there's the coherence you can see through

yes   tears fall incessant before the furnace
scald into quiet incandescence where
tears hiss and disappear
consumed back into air
tears corrode and sear
the night of the broken windows

yes   remember the glass bead makers   hands
'trembling with an exquisitely timed palsy'
who worked their lethal transparency in a sunless shed
fetid hours over the furnace
a juddering sickness estranged from hands
owned by baubles   a crystal drop
enclosing a trembling light   a
sensuous unstable tear   unbelievably
set hard   the sharp click and chock as they roll
in their hundreds
roll
to charm an African

yes   I remember   transparency   adiaphane
splinter at the heart   tears annealed in glass
the night of the broken windows
all that   but it still claims me
transparency   poetics
come away

2 IMAGES   VASE   IMAGES
angel rush of golden wings   burnished plumes
aureole radiance
burnished pinions
golden aura of an annunciation
incandescing surprise

will never return except
in transubstantiated secondary forms
imagined
as glass imagines images

a form of stone
to be seen through
glazed with its own inner tinctures
where crystalline surfaces
work with light
to figure limpid cavities
distances far inside
dreaming glass
unreachable coalescences of gleam and gold
seen through
far far inside
another land
of gold gleam glistening
seen through
another gleam
another gleams

sometimes it will interrupt
its reveries
to play jokes with the world
now reflecting a lambent yellow wall
shadow on the wall
against a bright blue sky
and then upside down
in another space
yellow wall and shadow
grounded in bluer sky
and distended at the curve of the vase
almost unseen
the yellow wall   shadow   blue sky   and
its elongated double   inverted
stretched at the bottom of the blue sky   yellow
wall shadow
at another curve

it plays with windows
reflecting windows

making an image of
what it is made of
by the stuff it is made of
the geometry of casement   and lattice
where faces gaze   waiting
for the lover's return   or simply
gazing   over the red geraniums that scald the air
and takes into itself   impartially
the street's spectacle   people living lives

its imaginings
or if he pleases through it pass and then the heaven espy

seeing through

what is through
through
sky reflected in glass
to sky beyond
through
the pallor of air and tense bare
branches imaged here
to the trees outside
dark-thonged tension of bare branches
in the act of mimesis
images throng
through
minuscule impediments
scratches   grazes   conglobed drops of air
annealed
inwardly trembling   undulations congealed
through
the curve of frozen breath
golden refractions quiver
configurations of light
out of light   figure
a quivering rainbow spectrum
that oscillates   and goes

through
images through
crossed with a gleam
of the onlooking self
inside and outside
now deep in internal cavities of transparency
now deep in branches tense and bare
in the outer air
through

onlooking self
fused in the imagination of glass

Alembic Sun

golden sun late lazy large and slow
ending day each day now hot now
warm now grasping at the later hour
willing the lees of light

golden sun to dark and on again
dawn fever rising from the night
hot skin burns and ice within sweats holds
willing the heat change fast

golden sun drawing out the heart beat
into pulse of time now stolen
breath after breath drawn from beaded thread
willing life and what's mine

gold rush midas stone philosopher's
blood touch alembic deeper red
mine blows changeling inflating to vein
I would not look for heart

gold rush surge the fluid and heat charge
all to crumbling merge ashes dearth
pulsing red crusted promising me
I would not look for calm

gold rush fiery dark red flowing
stir and pour look for more than hope
quick spurt sounds of a deeper flash charge
I would not look for life

you give it to me, give me more and
give me sun gold, heat life, relief
take away this deluding sickness
melt chilindre brand seal

you give it to me the darkness heal
count drops, hours, shade from blinding heat
error out terror out alchemise
pound the rays and forge me

you give it to me gild leaves leavings
beyond the pain of setting sun
repeat red sulphur gold cheating hope
grey weld and massicot

I tell you visions the furnace set
in leaden sky and blood congeals
shadows dispossess life cast
minted xanthin flowers

What We Have Seen ... Prevent/

when the body has been disintegrated
demobilised with an asymmetric threat
ring out the tattoo of relentless guns
on an embattled hilltop
you have us squarely in your sights
prevent such a death ... Deter /

when the body has been weaponised
the splinters of bone descend in a shower
but these have been rapidly neutralised
pull back the repeater and fire
into the valley where we have been cornered
deter such a terror... Coerce /

when the body has been disintegrated
deployed to a suicidal effect
wring out your tired hands and
in a zone where you thought you were safe
you decode us to a silent pause
coerce a survival... Disrupt/

when the body has been weaponised
interference produces maximum reach
we re-pole you and swear that
your human contents are contaminated
open up the sluices we need more clean water
disrupt the deformation... Destroy /

when the body has been disintegrated
use insistent medical agents
dry sandy soil and cracked houses
stand in our way shattered with
our stabilised insistent resurgence
destroy deterrent effect... check/
these neutralised splinters carry diseases... check/
sanity... check/
who are you... *check/*
have we enough....

David Greenslade

Prism Descent

What reason fless, extremity leads to sorrow   *Martin Sinaws*

Prisms bend the light of close relations,
assessing how a zip might split apart
should spirit overstuff with heat.

Fire isn't what it used to be now staircase
pulpits burst with every cause to burn,
foundations steam their hidden roots.

Arguments (cast well adrift from facts) defend
the herring action of a fabric hook,
certain of disguise by invading even more.

Toxic visits—high minded compromise
concedes a visceral hallucination gasp.
Suspicion modifies an ordinary aftermath.

Flying Buttress

Architecture is a theatre of social empathy   *Spiro Picolli*

More than my hand carries, completes
the life cycle of a trowel, it could be
cloth that simply makes a world tomorrow.

Scratch marks swell the wandering surface, hauliers
indicate which street unpacks a labyrinth—
guilds migrate from florid Gothic to Tudor caravan.

Chsiels ampliying stone repeat choral
thank loops under thumb, one foreman mutters,
not just this buttress our eager flights conceive.

The Other Table

Eavesdroping confirms how interesting horizons always are
                                        Hans Beckermann

Cynephoros pants for the coveted brew
and contaminates floral patterned cups,
when they bloom
a portly pundit storms his tea.

Choose another menu, should a food taboo
enter the canteen through layers of bruised fruit.
On open collar shirt frills coarse humour flashes
a formulaic joke while entering a pub. Command a pint.

You can bring that dog in here the suntan says. Games
roll double sixes and a butcher's van invites compassion fate.

Authorised endearments sigh, relax, depart
in a crumpled, origami boat—a normally
permitted topic stiffens when the fabric library
calls advantage on a low, corrosive note.

B

introducing	honey	the	**boy**
commands words	punches	holes in	doors
baltic **blue**	stakhanovite		my
nineteen year	old	heart speaks	in
socialist	economics		flips
when you	floor	the	**belorussian**
hollers out	**black**	sea	aquatics
synchronised	**beyond**	all	fetish

tender engines don't shunt

craving connection.
result of being
raised in earshot
of trains and railey
walls. rubber shoes keep
bouncing off the lines
into primary coloured
carriages. constant stair
crawling lift swapping
frantic platform dash.
i'd hate to miss you.

GARY HOTHAM

Four Haiku

before the day begins below freezing
easy to follow
instructions

birthday wishes
stones skipping across water
that isn't ours

before
the frost has a chance to melt
not a day to find myself

rain in the storm drain
new neighbors who haven't moved
the tulip bed

Alison Fraser

Blood Chit

I approach when he tells me I've forgot:
still skulls of horses, uncommon measurements
raw bone that against fire broke and was left
for woods to grow around, and the fence to fall
water remains in the old well at the curve of the brook
past the waterfall, so we found

haste beginning to the end, the aged plant that contains itself
the putting forth of teeth, iced roots that cannot do so at once
brought to close up, each becoming upwards in one being
now light in the grass at the base of the lawn
tightens its repose until she-balsam bark blisters
run from six branches' budded blooming lee-side lichens

I could say it was mine because I broke this body in it
and I watched her hands clutch and reclutch the empty air
lost from my chest, no reverberation to put nails to cheek
to undress my worry, now until this wind grows
long unto my arm measuring in block
'til I no longer know the way to my own foot

go into the right woods, so sweet and full
sometimes I can almost see, owned now adrift
I sat, ringed by a circle, and they said I would not know
the bare bone edges of my fingers curl beneath skin
loved by his churlish heart; I could not count how I've aged
I am without measurement and the snow comes but does not fall

On Both Sides

On the bald hill, where we killed three horses,
I can see the planes landing in the valley.
They will pass very close to this hill;
None of the men are afraid.
It seems sometimes that they are clouds,
Drafting right and left right behind.
There are reports that they are on the ground nearby.
On the back of the last horse, I get off this hill.

On the hill's northeast face, the women are bloodstained.
"When all is to forget beauty's decline,"
He says. Under these conditions,
I am quite happy to live in the basement room.
I kill two grouse out back and I will eat them.
I leave the feathers for leaves. My nails are ice.

from Archilochus on the Moon

8.

Zeus, a fucking sign
would be welcome, other

than your swap
of newly smith'd spears

for a spine.
Until then

I decline all offerings, place
no further bets

and if I'm still
your pet, be advised

I bite
even my own limbs;

what's mine, is yours:
a mouth full of blood

irrigates my pride,
sole lunar crop

9.

I speak ill, as
we've had our fill of Zeus-born kings
and Spartan heroes.

Sack the moon,
and you sack all
that lights the underside of Eros

stokes
those body-bits
that do the joining

and the mind
they favour and fever
riots like a market-place.

I have no love of tyranny.
Everything is for the Gods, so
they can have this:

Thanks

10.

Artemis, Selene and Hecate
you lunar three
owe me an explanation;

after this abysmal journey
to a land beyond coin and precinct
to where the Earth-stone sinks
below the horizon:

where should I find one
with whom to play
the sinews of my soft horn;

for it may yet
produce song
when skilfully played upon

still elevate
white
libations

11.

day, day, day
you stay so long here
sleep seems the wrong decision

even when, Earthshine-blind,
time itself freezes
glass discolours;

and we discover
nothing soft; no waves
have played rocks
to pebbles

not a single snowflake
shapes these peaks,
yet our feet are winged

things change weight;
a thrown feather
outstrips a heavier vessel

and we no longer wrestle
with the packs on our backs
being Olympian

on this heap of stones

ANNE GORRICK

Atomica across the water with a Morpheus action figure
(after poem 'Lady Catfish' —as suggested by Google)

The butcher says, "It's anime snacktime!"
Ghostman, frost, monkeywrestle Montreal
Hunt for mushrooms in a morphine galaxy that looks like New Jersey
False freezing, then fried in butter
A flock of dimes, a mansard roof vampire weekend
Her mansion is taller than mine
A widow's walk, her tears diverted on multiple slopes
When multiplying exponents on instapaper
Medicine got it wrong when memory dies
Melted chocolate makes you thinner
When melody is ripe and in season
Dolphin infused vodka, insect into select
Insert pearls into an oracle, and then turn a lemon into a battery
A mason is about to expose all his secrets
Tajikistan stupidly, a mirror for Perseus, a catalyst
Almost b, barely c
His holiness's petroleum is limited
Molarity, my mouth with myriad subtitles, bankrupted commas
A panic-ed atheism in salmon damask
The heart's curriculum
Mandarin oranges, my prophet chunders
She wears her depression mascara and
watches Madagascar penguins in a Christmas caper
Wax butterflies with the cutest personalities
Hungrynowhere, under a wrecking ball moon
The rage written in the from and to on an envelope
Igloos sewn with human summary
An example of a nonelectrolyte event
An elm and three sisters, pollen mixed with transit
The disease in this phrase, sleep strapped to his friendly attachments
Philadelphia's sunny disintegration
An alarm clock that actually cooks bacon
A nerdist breakdown in itchy bumps, in Japanese

Hexidecimal Hawaiian Hindusim
He is comprised of a repeating self, his best sarcastic gospel
Saran wrap weight loss for wufniks
Abandon the heart as if it were a florist
Salt means help or luck
A mouth full of gold, many of his attributes are not valid
A memory of light, or a chest to pin a medal on

Damn you, autocorrect
Damsel lace, ladder rungs
A dictionary burial at sea
Swallow death in a sentence, its ice green lava
Program logic rattles and gnarls
A maneating and stock picking robot
A parade of oyster and theories
I should be in French, where the days are divided by a darkroom
        discretion
He was finally alone with his digital dream materials, his dudeness,
        his divine shadow
Random number generator, ransom note generator
Android tourists sleeping for intensive purposes
Her headache was high in fat in her manorama
Biblebirds, a relative's DNA like an omen machine
Plum oil, a jam colored shawl when the sun turns blue
Bacon oracle bioavailability, kiss midnight from mouth to ear
Tanning luminosity in pythagoreanism
George Bataille, sonically speaking, said
Arsonists get all the girls
Say a novena to make darkness fall, to kiss girls
Hybridize that sonata, note that her realm is closed but can be visited
Use this poem to generate random events
Randomly firing freeze ray, throwing up, falling asleep, losing weight
Stop breathing, you are a fortune cookie cliché in Vasoline, Taco
        Bell meat, urine

Poem

1.

Lip-locked,
place-ridden.

Happenstance casts
a cork anchor—
incision
into the closed parentheses

> (as chance may have it,
> may not,
> may leave it open—)

a painless surgery on the ever-
healing-over

eventlessness.
Counterfeit coins of days—
small change,
loose change:

> alms to myself, begging
> at the corners of long
> afternoons.

Eye
caught up in reflections (mis)
-carries the *ever*
along the two-weeks' diameter,
immobilizes in
monologues

the Host to one's lips'
partedness.

Full stop splits into colon:
casts the dice
to unlace the street lights,
to step in—barely leave
ruins,

                    (a shortcut of the
                    two weeks' radius).

Else,
to step out:
a name—less,
initials, less—
a letter:

silhouette, mired
knee-deep in mirrors
(a static railway-ever-
-go-round,

from here
into here in your side
vision,
via the *Schwarzenberggasse*).

2.

Home relics
counterspell:

an essay proof-
read by a deaf hand,
sealed in, powdered with
dust.

At daybreak
waters lie seamless,
straitjacketed with eleven bridges.
One waits for winter,
face-prints on the pane.

Full stops crumble to marks of omission.

                              (and the mist turns yesterday
                              by osmosis. Yesterday's
                              hollow hours' holy minutes
                              of Lent and Carnival, blood and roses).

Months siblings, hole-
bellied—a
yellow light stutter at the crossing.
A monosyllabic stutter.
Place names,
lipped, silenced, are
locked away in the cupboards.
The stale yields no longer
to blade—

                              crumbles
                              to a forgetful sweep.

3.

Pivoted on desertion
the moons swing back—spill
over the cherry-striped coach.

Gypsies come,
predict your foresight,
carry away the moons—
leave behind
one
to play solitaire to
with your pack of *cartes blanches.*

The words-split, a greyhaired beetle,
is shaping
lips: open, closed, open
brackets.

Awake, you see the railway slit
your hemi-
sphered vision.

ANDREW MCMILLAN

just because I do this   doesn't mean

not knowing names doesn't make it something less
the midroad fight over red jumper and bike doesn't make it
something more   it was just

    a long walk through see saw streets
    a stomach stretched tight as drumskin over hollow abdomen
    mouths finding every part of one another

    watching the mirror like a laptop screen
    a moon that kept trying to light us but kept off
    a flat full of shortflightstopover

    the one who wanted to pretend he was wrestling
    to be pinned under the anxious face of the clock   watching
    the kisses that wanted to stay for longer than a night

    the one who said he wants to be a writer
    in the way an old woman in slippers
    might say she used to want to be a dancer

    the heavy scent of them as they showered and I dressed
    running until I was breathless in the centre of town
    it wasn't the rain   the rain hadn't come yet   but it would

gospel

this is not the beginning
of a joke
two monks get on a train
one says to the other
and what I take from that is that I don't really have to change at all
outside a lake is frozen thick enough to walk on

morn

the night is clouding
trees   shadow   nighttrain
Manchester is growing out towards us

the night is raining
fields   go   unrisen
act like you're not waiting

the night is only briefly shining
feralfruit   gloves   empty house
the birthdays of the dead become unseemly

the night is not so much clouding as burying itself

standard class

on a train   hot from the wet outside   a man opposite
reads a student's dissertation   embossed on the cover   the words
Bergen Belsen   liberation gender and aftermath
the writing is gold against the black cover and the man
goes straight to the bibliography   and nods twice
and I imagine him   behind a lectern   saying history needs its
proper witnesses
and as he returns it to its bag I see a book   *fractured loyalties*
I misread as *fractured love*

Lynne Hjelmgaard

In the music of wind and water

Cross currents lift and roll Annalise.
Plankton, fellow wanderer, twirls and sways.
One hand for the ship!

I sit at an angle in a secure corner
alone on watch, my feet braced
against the bulkhead.

Check forward then aft, harnessed
to the cleat, as my husband sleeps below,
I ward off any dangers:

an approaching freighter,
a roving oil drum,
a freak wave that could swamp

the cockpit or black clouds
lingering too long,
like vessels that echo loss.

On a clear and windless day
we lazy about, enjoy our breakfast,
do a spring clean below.

In the music of wind and water,
our bodies shift to a living-on-land mode
and forget, for a few hours
or days even, who and where we are.

We have free run about the cabin,
no lurching for grab-holds or
struggles with a sloping loo.

Our spirits lift and open
as we glare at our reflections
in the smooth surface azure.

It looks back at us knowingly.
Connected to the universe,
disconnected from the world.

Novice

Annalise plows through the wind's eye,
beating in a blow.
The mast vibrates, sails flutter
until settled or are tightened
to lie flat. Lines snap,
shrouds hum, the hull leans over
as insolent waves water
the deck or us.

After all this
Annalise is in the same exact spot.
Foul weather gear
is too heavy to wear.
And even worse to shed it,
if one dares go below.
(The wretched lurching up and down.)

This is a washing machine.
I am turned inside out.
My husband can crawl on deck
while seas wash over him,
take sails down,
mend them
when they tear,
repair the engine, the rigging, the head
and at the same time, cook.

When first offshore
I stare at my own fear-shadow
for what feels like days upon days,
until I realize I still exist;
the seas are endurable,
my nausea has disappeared.

My husband knows I will come around.
Be counted on for my watch,
report anything suspect.
But we are edging closer,
I feel it.
The more difficult
to reach, the stronger
the sense and
longing for land.

How precious a thing
to lie steady,
snug and warm.
The pleasure of
a small island
with a spit of sand
to wake you
by its mere presence.

Seeing, Believing

Erasmus was wrong: when you turn on the light
darkness reinvents itself as shadow

Your shadow is uniquely yours
but looks like everyone else

A grope in the dark sounds fun
but not if nothing's there

Those guys in Plato's cave
trust their imagination

Scared of the night and a candle in the hand
watch those dreams escape from sleep, and be believed

as when sunlight strikes the steel of mortal men in battle
soldiers seem like angels

Seawatcher

The skilled seawatcher
looks first to the sky

source of all its trauma
and desire

next the wind,
breaker of moods

must bow to the moon,
god of every move

reads the surface like a play
holding a mirror to infinity

knows that what cannot be seen
is what matters most

keeps all options open:
the stillness of a dancer, coiled,

the frenzy of a dreamer, dazzled
by the brightness of fog

leans into the wind, standing
on the cliff's very edge

fingering the brokem, blood-crusted
stump of hill, breaking still

Westron Wynde

Leaf and branch shrieking
wind ripping, tearing

wave after wave breaking
like fists on a prison door.

I hunker down behind a flint wall
to hear secrets whispered low

troubled love, broken hope
lust and rage unbound

listen like a priest in his box
agog at so much wildness

longing to come back as snow
blown across the fell

Pointed Remarks

1. TO GUARD AGAINST CONFUSION, PLEASE SAY NOTHING

Talking isn't really my thing
but let's give it a go:
Love is a spiral staircase—
enticing, staggering, impossibly steep.
It makes me giddy.
Stop laughing!
The future is only a brief stop.

2. DON'T BE SO TOUCHY

And you? Have you been waiting long?
This is the polecats' favourite place at night.
One thing's clear:
it won't be a walk in the park.

Good plan! I'll behave!
Just hypothetically—
is everything under control?

3. SILENCE IN COURT

You're looking rough
though I'm the victim in this story.
I thought about you the whole way here.

No need to be embarrassed.
Have you been reading Henry James?

The wild boar is furtive and conscientious,
he gets under your skin.

Victim—good catchword!
The pleasure was all mine.
Another round?
No further questions.

4. THE SAME AS BEFORE, ONLY WITHOUT STRAY DOGS

You kept your word: it doesn't hurt.
But something smells risky,
something smells burnt.

5. KILL-JOY

The mating call of the short-eared owl is
irresistible. Such a show-off,
so sanctimonious, so pious.
I grind my teeth,
I stiffen like dry rot.

You know what's a shame?
I had other choices:
the fortune-cookie could have been swapped.

Just for the record—
were we on familiar terms?

6. THE THING ABOUT FATE

I've been off the rails
since birth.
It's a long trek: mis-
understandings, dis-
agreements, Beauty
and the Beast…

Oh, collapsible love!
How do you imagine it?
The fact is—
I must—
And that's my final word.

SONIA OVERALL

Richter's Paris

there is something in the way that dust settles

you do not want to look down
but the tail of your eye
is drawn by the crumpled, lidless boxes

shameless   roofless
exposing their slotted innards to the skies

for a second you glimpse   a bathtub   drawn water waiting

but that cannot be

against the drone of the engine
the words: *what happened here?*

you cough awkwardly

nobody answers

Margate, 5th May

You make a pilgrimage to Hamish Fulton's milestones and full-moon walks. Old straight tracks and forced courses. In the cube of the gallery you shuffle at the perimeter, safety in short distances, your own termite walk. You feel as if you are participating.

An object cannot compete with an experience. Even so, you linger over the smuggled Tibetan flag, hungry for reliquary.

You are enamoured with text. There is a pleasurable hollowness in your belly, like the spaciousness after a fever. Then a toddler breaks in, squeals at the giant red SILENCE on the wall, gleefully stamps in orange boots. You realise that she is participating.

The tide is high, swollen by twelve days of rain. The harbour arm struggles to contain it.

Flitting between galleries, you think: there is as much in a straight-trodden line as in any Turner firebomb. Visitors cluster before a furnace. No matter how you resist you are drawn to the light, the slow goosestep of the figurative.

That night your dreams are of levitation, of a marching bass, of an endless single line of yellow road-paint cutting through the Downs.

NORMAN JOPE

Friedrich in the Forest

Traces of a wolf—and of a soldier, peering
through the paint of his eyes in mid-afternoon.
There's something afoot that turns this world to winter,
a trick of the light when seen through pines
and, on the snow-covered slope, a cross
drives a stake through industriousness and noise.
I enter the canvas, dreaming as I breathe.
The unconfined takes the shape of clouds
and the world's renewed with its excellence of birds.

I enter the canvas, breathing as I dream
and as hushed as the land is. A pilgrim
into snow-depth and star-cloud, I seek strange light
from without and within, writing down my footprints
as I deepen in, lost foundling like that soldier
from a confident southern army. What ate him, wolf or bear?
No matter. By spring, his jawbone had bleached.
The birds are simply and elusively themselves
and the unconfined takes the shape of clouds.

By the spring, his jawbone had bleached
but, on a mild green slope, I replace that cross
and know that, all around, the world has changed
to a new form of light. Industriousness and noise
are useless commodities where life's this simple
and something too innocent for godhood lurks
like a starving wolf. The deeper in, the more I praise.
I have entered the canvas, dreaming as I sing
and there is nothing I need that is not from the forest.

Ice on the Stylus

Amon Düül II, Yeti

On the K2 or Dachstein. a peppermint snow-cool intro
heralds a masculine shape with fur the colour of silver
you need crampons to dig. In a Munich studio
they case each other's joints, these wary musicians

as the raga begins to move, from Ganges to Kailas,
from Schwabing to the methane sheen of Triton—
his antimony shadow's cast across night
as taxis growl off set, as Andreas and Gudrun

skulk in myths of divine retribution
expressed in broken glass and an equally-jagged
glamour fix. He walks by way of this music
into Bavarian pastures, half-iced, like Herzog

striding to oppose a death that did not happen—
for what is ahead, in this place and time
is all tomorrow. Opels and Porsches
race from the foul paternal darkness

into a place the blood friends mapped
six centuries before. What restlessness, what ambition
is encoded here. A being like an iceberg, like a mineral Golem
strides, beyond the TV towers and stage-set precincts

into steppe-space and space-steppe, into all wind hurls...
and slows to percussive applause. A bass motif repeats
and we are on the plateau. It is 1971, with infinite oil
and a glorious hubris we lack. Note by exultant note

                he crosses our path once more.

A Faustian Spiral

improvisations to the music of Faust

1. BEYOND THE MERELY POSSIBLE (SO FAR, SIDE ONE)

A sunshine girl is being rained on.
They are beating on my heart, said Krag,
with rubber hammers. With toffee hammers
when in lenient mood. But we leave him to groan
and it's off to Adamäe, a place on a map
that melts in the mouth to the softest of guitars
played slowly, in the evening, by a brook
between aspens. And what if it can't be found?
The magic of those evenings, somehow
it must still exist, it was not that long ago
and death, for what it's worth, is only the errand-boy
of entropy. In nostalgia for what is possibly not
we travel, my inner Bavarian hippie and I
through clouds of Acapulco smoke.
No harm in that, we are told to take the banana
and it's Sunday tomorrow, after all,
Herr Schmidt has returned from his shift
and parks his Audi. Wirtwunderschaft!
I exclaim, in a howl, but Herr Schmidt only frowns
as Frau Schmidt polishes the steps of their heimat.
Make music to silence the past, to overwhelm
the sweet schlagermusik, declaimed from hillsides
to the living rooms of the Ruhr. The banana, squeezed,
explodes and scatters the showroom dummies
and a communiqué lives on. I wave to the astronauts
and practice free love, by myself, in a spray-painted room
to the sound of wild beasts, disguised as musicians
on an evening, long ago, on the plains south of Hamburg.
So many possibilities, I think. I will go to my grave
in the dustbin thinking this delicious thought.

There are twangs from a low industrial horizon
where trains purr. On four-leaf clovers
the insatiable traffic heads for Utopia.
I skank to a pseudo-reggae rhythm
in a shoal of seagulls, listening to the clank
of commerce and machinery, on a lowering day
that meant business from the beginning.
We have come so far, I think, from the ruins
and women bearing bricks in baskets
and eye patch soldiers limping towards them
and the occupiers' leering eyes—
once more, our conurbations are huge
and clean as skulls left out in the sun
and our music, these days, is as loud
as an ultrasound we have charmed from void.
Mamie and Daddy are blue as they listen
to the side-burned magus on the far-seen screen.
I watch from both within and above,
the city vast on the plain, the space
that pours in from the east like an army,
and I am lacking everything but space,
in the spirit I'm still huge, a presence stretching
down threads of asphalt and canals,
past suburban precincts and lock-ups
to the ultravoid. Rain, ghosts, the lure of a fuck
with a hollow-eyed avatar, the Tarot spread
on her soft red duvet, even in sleep
and in tangled limbs of enamoured sleepers
the tribes are on the move. It is 1972
and Rimbaud's prescription has been claimed.
We are utterly modern, in magnetic lives.

3. PIANO MILK (THE FAUST TAPES, SIDE ONE)

A pastoral is also an excursion. By the power-lines
heifers graze, pianos snort, no-one can tell the difference
and the revolution, un-televised, begins on the plain
of Niedersachsen, electrifying beetroots.
I want to wake up there, tomorrow morning
as if I had never been away. But sideburns, blond afros
and Afghans, dodgy muesli and thoughts of fraternity
and free love falter. I am borne into the vortex
where trucks howl, into which the great
industrial estates are bulging and the Lego
suburbs. And in this city that is a cat's cradle
of Brutalist energy, the words go zigzag and yet,
I think I can make them out. I am in a bar
on a crumbling corner, ROCK OFF says the jukebox
playing the music that it makes for itself.
Two thugs in expensive coats
hassle a whore and an ingénue looks on.
Pianos strut, stopping the traffic.
This assault is pitiless, it breaks the speed-limit,
racing over statues, blonde gods in the earth
and columns. Everywhere is as glass, including
our souls. The speaking clock's our oracle. Now is not
tomorrow afternoon, it is a rush of melted sugar
and amphetamine. Is our hero, rushing
from city to city in the snatch of a song that explodes
from a turned-up radio. Thirty years from the Hitlerjugend,
the achieved society, fast food on the hoof, Imbiss snacks
and petrol-station beer. Everything cross-cut with everything,
citywithcity, wavebandwithwaveband, passionwithpassion…
ROCK OFF! Again. We dance at the feet of a god
who tells us that his music must be made with power-drills.

We sidle through fields to a farmhouse
overgrown with wires, shaking with noise
from Saxon window to window.
Half-timbered hall where heroes
no longer lurk, you resonate!
Deep blues from the unimaginable Delta
lick this far, fragment into glissando
hundreds and thousands. The aim's
to tease out every nuance of sound,
to exhaust the catalogue and retire
to the road that still leads out, the endless miles
of this country, its truck stops
and its malls. It is to wake each morning
in a different town, completely exposed
and drink the same coffee, only that.
A tribe detached from the heroic past
explores the future, turning it to present
and the music's its mark. A metronome
counts days, the politicians arrange the deckchairs
and the miracle, taken for granted at last,
begins to look threadbare. What a place in which
to lay down tracks, as the dazzling form of an aircraft
expresses the jet-set mythos. We are innocent
in our guile, we have no knowledge
of a yesterday that slavers and barks
in equal measure. Free-born nomads with credit cards
we praise with affectionate scorn. This heimat's
a map, swept up from the carpet into cloud
that follows us on our journey - on a clear day,
we can sense the Urals, not a hint of dread to be seen.
Over the forgotten avalanche we stride,
always whistling riffs of our own devising.

David Miller

Spiritual Letters (Series 6, #7)

She told me that as a little girl she thought of spiders as her friends
and would read stories to them. *Did the other children call you Spider
Girl?* I wondered, hoping that they didn't. The Persian rugs displayed
outside the café drew the eye as surely as the hookah pipes. Was
it then or some other time that she mentioned a hankering for
hookah-smoking?

> foreshortening
> your face here there here
> foreshadowing
>
> - - - -
>
> *in dark looking out*
> four hours past midnight
> cathedral glass blue
> above the white
> wooden shutters

I shook the old piece of chocolate out of the trap—a trap already
baited but which I had added bait to—into a rubbish bag; but as
I did I noticed the small dark shape had a tail, and realised I
had something to rescue and release. —I've made a breakthrough,
he told me; I'm no longer afraid of the mouse in my flat. —There's
someone here with a strong body odour, she said as we entered the
gallery; I replied that I couldn't detect anything. —Yes, she continued,
I have a really good sense of smell; my mother and I can both smell
snakes. An apple tree in blossom, with a lone squirrel negotiating
the branches. The two fox cubs jumped over each other, tussled,
exposing their bellies, and ran back and forth in the garden; one
found an abandoned yellow plastic toy to play with, and every time
it picked it up in its jaws the toy let out a squeak. My philosophy
tutor introduced me to her cat, Pascal, and then to her pet rabbit,
but without telling me its name (—It's too embarrassing, she said).
I had been thinking it might be called Spinoza or Kierkegaard,
but she eventually told me it was Bun-bun. Hail beating, crashing,

battering against the windows and roofs as I sit in a room upstairs overlooking the garden, writing to a friend; the white stones covered the grass and the long beds of soil. A dog bitten on the face by a rattler survived; a different dog was bit on the leg and died. —Why did he leave his dead dog out in the woods to rot—and what did he really expect his friends to say when they encountered it? The storm hit, as sudden as the rain and wind were violent; he hysterically chased around the rooms of his house arranging buckets and saucepans, with little sense that I could see. I stood there astonished at his panic, as I really thought I'd seen worse in my own country. You claimed that the colour of your eyes had recently changed, and that the brown irises had become tinged with red. But I'd never allowed myself to look closely enough before; and I refrained from doing so now. The lashing rain obscured the streetlamp outside my window. Water dripped from the ceiling while, oblivious, he talked on the phone. —Is there anything I can carry for you, dear one? I know you don't have socks or a pocket watch, but the water is deep, and there must be something I could carry.... When I heard that someone had dropped ten thousand poems from a helicopter, I could easily imagine that she'd been the pilot, as well as one of the poets. No way of asking her, however, as she'd completely stopped speaking to me. —It's the sea that the heart lives on, and the sea is salt; it's salt the heart lives on. A stark ark. Often one by one, and none by none at times. Wind, hail, heavy rain, thundersnow... heart's beat. *Then,* he wrote, *it all stopped: she stopped painting, he stopped living, I couldn't continue writing, you and I stopped....* Please tell me *no.*

Spiritual Letters (Series 6, #8)

We had sat down to rest when darkness fell, not the dark of a moonless or cloudy night, but as if the lamp had been put out in a closed room. The young girl dreamt that she was walking down a stairway with the leader of the country, and that they chatted amiably together and all was well, all was pleasant, despite her grandmother's Jewish name. —Fairies may fool you into thinking they're your natural offspring; but one supposed father woke to the deception and put the alien child, now six, on a bed of burning coals to die. Another changeling was deposited with a human family during a tornado; after he reached adulthood, he built himself a studio and became the town photographer. *A gleam of light returned, but we took this to be a warning of the approaching flames rather than daylight.*

> though my best friend
> he shot at me
> as well as the others
> shooting all around
> I begged him begged and begged
> ----
> struck struck through
> he was struck down
> struck with a cane
> struck cut beaten

To release what was in his grasp upon death, it proved necessary to break the fingers. Could the words on paper dropped from the sky have been secret messages, telling of disappearances and deaths? Were a thousand and two hundred Jews waiting to converge on Giza and place a Star of David on top of the Great Pyramid? *The intricate lead crystal window above the door crashed into the street and pieces of furniture came flying through doors and windows.* —Separate out, he commanded. —No, I replied. *The subjugated should be left nothing but eyes for weeping.* —Anything, anything whatsoever you wish: anything's possible, everything you desire is permissible. —Can you walk through closed doors and walls, leap from a window high above the ground without injury, fly by your own agency… and what if you could, you who aren't capable of performing an act of compassion? Still in his army uniform, having just returned from being a prisoner-of-war, he stood in the middle, leaning his arms on the others' shoulders; and all three of them trying to look like *bad boys*, cigarettes in their mouths, cocky poses.... And I'd remembered sweat stains under their arms, all three of them, but the photograph gives this the lie. When news of the approaching army reached you, you shut the remaining prisoners in the mess and set the building alight; and those who managed to break out were met with flame-throwers and machine guns. He chose to jump from the ship that had been set ablaze, and swim amongst and past corpses in the freezing water. —You either burn or you swim; but if you decide to swim, you'll be shot at: because you're a Jew. Spark, flame, smoke... skip, trip, stop.

SYLVIA GEIST   *TRANSLATED BY CATHERINE HALES*

Germanium

I.
small quantities
widespread deficiency diseases are unknown likewise the benefits
for the organism a little too much affects the
    kidneys the outcome of respiratory paralysis is known. this
is product information: no

data reported
from studies on healthy subjects but undeniable deployments
in other areas. should one see through walls and
    in darkness on the hunt it'll hit the fifty
fifty again double twofold

hanging tight
to branches horse-hair or simply in the nature
of fellow-travellers yesterday to b who complained no business
    like you know and I didn't know where we
were in the woods.

II.

verdigris eating
at sheeting plasterwork the nonethelessnice on a course
that no-one's likely to envy you for slowing down
    next stop already. delayed arrival in stendal soon
enough off elsewhere. nowhere

have I
seen dahlias like in the garden that replaced
the one I was looking for quince scent reminding
    me of nothing made me sneeze in the renamed
street. I'd tossed a

small coin
to decide then over the fence. nearby someone
was chopping invisible timber. I heard him splitting stacking
    splitting the logs heard them drumming from the block
and nearly called out.

Tantalum

almost assuaged
what the day's paraded. crackling as fields fold
into each other outside inside swapping of heading for
     sale for wanted. make-believe grammar practised on soft prices
free-falling with hand-signs few questions about the ellipses'
       embarrassing secret: not wanted enough because too second-hand
too used. read-off: separated again without consensus evening's
       glowing thread shredded as below the sternum its
morse a menetekel that still surpasses your mind's horizon kilo by
kilo about

the brow
wadding for the muddle of crossings. waiting. wading.
constantly under fire from the transparent body of the
       next question please as though it were going somewhere
so it's all about spineless thirst and thus
       setting the organ's pace. connection! inflow! more air
than blood in the blood the swim-bladder sewn
     to the diseased place displeasing your gods but:
now you must be able to want to be undecided again
as cumulus

homunculus comical
acrobat you'll threaten. rage. stand. you'll look towards
the mirror. waving whitecoats. beg. look: their winking. white
     slits. you ought to know that nights demand amplitudes
around the sweet green waveline of systolic storms
     in the chest's container flickering when the heart
winds its strings in diagrams. bobbing puddle pisshole
     mouth admit it: what would you do what
not. the blinking again. the current. as though you weren't about
to sink.

New and Recent Titles from Shearsman

The Marvels of Lambeth
Interviews & Statements by Allen Fisher

edited by
Andrew Duncan

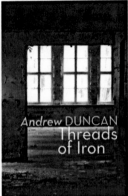

Andrew DUNCAN
Threads
of Iron

Andrew DUNCAN
In Five Eyes

poems

Alexandra Sashe
Antibodies

poems

John Matthias

Collected Shorter Poems

Vol. 1
1961–1994

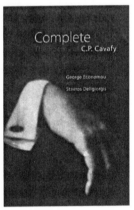

Complete
C.P. Cavafy

George Economou
Stavros Deligiorgis

Kelvin Corcoran

For the Greek Spring

Endtimes
Alan Wall

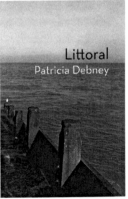

Littoral
Patricia Debney

Notes on Contributors

Isobel Armstrong is Emeritus Professor of English at Birkbeck, University of London and a Senior Research Fellow of the Institute of English Studies at the University of London, and is a Fellow of the British Academy. She is a specialist in 19th-century poetry, literature and women's writing. Her publications include *The Radical Aesthetic* (2000), *Women's Poetry, Late Romantic to Late Victorian: Gender and Genre* (1999) and *Victorian Poetry: Poetry, Politics and Poetics* (1993). Her poetry has appeared previously in *Shearsman* and in the anthology *Infinite Difference* (Shearsman, 2010).

Tom Bamford is a poet, writer, musician and proofreader based in London. His work has appeared in *Hi Zero* and is forthcoming in *Kaffeeklatsch*. He is the co-writer (with Jack Lowe) of the contemporary music piece *separate cat facilities*. Among other things he is opposed to Early Day Motion 912. Other activities can be followed at byproductions.tumblr.com.

Geraldine Clarkson also had work in the last issue. Her work has been appearing in a number of UK magazines, including Tears in the Fence, Smiths Knoll and Eyewear, and two pieces were featured in *This Line is not for Turning: Anthology of Contemporary British Prose Poetry,* (Cinnamon Press, 2011).

M.A. (Mary) Coghill lives in Devon. Her collection *Designed to Fade* was published by Shearsman in 2006. A new collection, *Shades of Light,* is out this year from the new publisher, City of Poetry.

Susan Connolly lives in Drogheda, Ireland. Her second collection, *Forest Music* was published by Shearsman in 2009. Recent publications have been in *Poetry Ireland Review, The Stony Thursday Book* and *Shine On: Irish Writers for Shine.*

Jen Crawford is originally from New Zealand, but now lives in Singapore, where she teaches at Nanyang Technological University. In 2000 Five Islands Press published her poetry sequence, *Admissions,* which was shortlisted for the Anne Elder and Dame Mary Gilmore awards. Her other publications include *bad appendix* (Auckland: Titus Books, 2009), *Napoleon Swings* (Auckland: Soapbox Press, 2009), and *Pop Riveter* (Auckland: Pania Press, 2011).

Sarah Crewe lives in Liverpool. Her first chapbook, *Aqua Rosa,* was released by erbacce press in 2012. Work is forthcoming in *The Sheffield Anthology: Poems From The City Imagine*d from Smith/Doorstop.

Anamaría Crowe Serrano has a collection from Shearsman, *Femispheres* (2008). She is a widely-published translator from Spanish and Italian, and lives in Dublin.

Alison Fraser is a PhD student studying poetics at the University at Buffalo.

SYLVIA GEIST is a Berlin-born poet and artist now based in Lower Saxony. She has won several prizes, has edited an anthology of Polish poetry, and has published several books, most recently *Der Pfau*, a novella (Vienna: Luftschacht Verlag, 2008), and a collection of poems *Vor dem Wetter* (Luftschacht, 2009).

ANNE GORRICK has three collections from Shearsman: *Kyotologic* (2008), *I-Formation (Book 1)* (2010) and *I-Formation (Book 2)* (2012). She lives in New York's Hudson Valley.

DAVID GREENSLADE's most recent collection is the Shearsman volume *Lyrical Diagrams* (2012). The poems here come from a developing collection called *Rarely Pretty Reasonable*, in which every poem will have an artwork on the facing page. He also writes in Welsh.

HARRY GUEST has a collected poems, *A Puzzling Harvest*, from Anvil, as well as a subsequent volume, *Some Time*. Shearsman published *Comparisons & Conversions* in 2008, a volume consisting of a long poem and a number of translations. *High on the Downs. A Festschrift for Harry Guest* was published by Shearsman to celebrate his 80th birthday in 2012.

CATHERINE HALES lives in Berlin and is a professional translator. Shearsman published her first collection *hazard or fall* in 2010.

BEN HICKMAN teaches at the University of Kent. He has two volumes of critical work from Edinburgh University Press: *Poetry and Real Politics: Crisis and the US Avant-Garde* (2013) and *John Ashbery and English Poetry* (2012).

LYNNE HJELMGAARD has a collection from Shearsman, *The Ring* (2011). She lives in Sussex.

NORMAN JOPE has a collection from Shearsman, *Dreams of the Caucasus* (2010), and two recent books from Waterloo Press: *The Book of Bells and Candles* (2009) and *Aphinar* (2012). He lives in Plymouth.

NINA KARACOSTA lives in Paris.

JOHN LATTA lives in Michigan. His first collection, *Rubbing Torsos*, appeared from Ithaca House in 1979. More recent is *Breeze*, winner of the 2003 Ernest Sandeen Prize in Poetry, from the University of Notre Dame Press. He blogs regularly at *Isola di Rifiuti*.

MAITREYABANDHU has a first collection, *The Crumb Road*, forthcoming from Bloodaxe, which has been selected as a Poetry Book Society Recommendation for the second quarter of 2013. He teaches at the London Buddhist Centre, and was ordained into the Western Buddhist Order 20 years ago. A chapbook *The Bond* appeared from Smith/Doorstop in 2011 and was shortlisted for the Michael Marks Award. His poems have won a number of prizes, and have been widely published in British journals. He has also published two books on Buddhism.

ANDREW MCMILLAN teaches Creative Writing at Liverpool John Moores University. His work has appeared in *The Salt Book of Younger Poets* and in two chapbooks: *protest of the physical*, due from Holdfire Press in late 2013, and *the moon is a supporting player* (Red Squirrel Press).

DAVID MILLER's collected prose, *The Waters of Marah* (2006) is available from Shearsman in the UK and Singing Horse Press in the USA. A large volume of his poetry is in the planning stages. Parts of the *Spiritual Letters* project have appeared in a Reality Street volume of the same name.

PAUL O'PREY is Vice-Chancellor of Roehampton University and an authority on the work of Robert Graves, whose correspondence and essays on poetry he has edited. He has also co-translated Emilia Pardo Bazán's novel *The House of Ulloa* for Penguin, and has seen his poetry appear in a number of UK magazines.

SONIA OVERALL teaches part-time at the University of Kent, and is a novelist, with two books published by Fourth Estate: *A Likeness* (2005) and *The Realm of Shells* (2011).

SIMON PERRIL lives in Rutland and teaches at De Montfort University, Leicester. The poems in this issue come from his forthcoming Shearsman volume, *Archilochus on the Moon*. His most recent collection was *Nitrate* (Salt Publishing, Cambridge, 2010).

SAM SAMPSON lives in Auckland. Shearsman co-published his first collection *Everything Talks* (2008) with Auckland University Press. One of the poems from his last appearance in this magazine was selected as one of the best New Zealand poems of 2012.

ALEXANDRA SASHE is a poet, linguist and translator. She is a regular contributor to literary reviews in the UK, France and Austria. Born in Moscow, she spent her most formative years in Paris. Following the swerve her personal life and her poetics were taking—towards Germanic culture— she has recently moved to Vienna, where she now lives. Shearsman Books published her first collection, *Antibodies*, in April 2013.

SIRIOL TROUP's last collection was the Shearsman volume, *Beneath the Rime* (2009). She lives in Twickenham.

TAMAR YOSELOFF lives in London, is a freelance creative-writing tutor, and has published four collections, most recently *The City with Horns* (2011) and *Fetch* (2007), both from Salt Publishing. She divides her time between London and Suffolk.

Lightning Source UK Ltd.
Milton Keynes UK
UKOW041221250413

209754UK00001B/2/P